101 THINGS TO KNOW PRIOR TO TAKEOFF

TRAVEL GUIDE FOR NEW AGENTS AND DIY'ERS

CHERYL CUFFE

ISBN: 978-1-928155-71-3

PUBLISHED BY:
10-10-10 PUBLISHING
MARKHAM, ON
CANADA

Contents

Dedication

This book is dedicated to all those who desire an unlimited income while doing what they love to do.

Acknowledgments

I would not have been able to write this book if it wasn't for the knowledge I received over the past 26 years in the Travel Industry. I thank my college and all the fantastic destinations and people I worked with that contributed to my experience.

Foreword

Cheryl Cuffe has used her vast experience with Fortune 500 companies to give you a great understanding of the Travel Industry from which you can dive into your new career or better understand your DIY adventure.

By using this detailed guide and bonuses, she introduces you to cruises, destination weddings, the benefits of booking groups for you and your clients and much more.

She goes through all the necessary information you will need in your day to day career. This is all done for the cost of a travel industry service fee while saving you thousands of dollars in tuition costs.

Raymond Aaron
Author and Success Coach

Bonuses are available at
www.priortotakeoff.com

1
Check In

- Introduction to Travel and Tourism
- Industry Lingo
- Getting to know your client

Great, you have decided to make your career something you love to do anyway. Get ready to discover how you and your clients can travel for FREE!! Of course you will have to read further to discover how you can do that. Have you thought of how much you would like your income to be? Your income can be unlimited you know. You decide how much you would like to earn, it's really that simple. Now let's begin….

Travel and Tourism is the largest industry in the world. It is responsible for the main source of income in many countries around the world. There are many branches of the industry including Hospitality (hotels and food and beverage), Conventions, Retail Travel Agents, Wholesalers, Suppliers and others yet they are all interconnected. In this book we are going to concentrate on the role of a Travel Agent and give you the knowledge you need to become one or at least have the information they have access to so you can Do-It-Yourself (DIY)

Since the invention of the internet, it has become much simpler for a person to book their own trip. however what they once thought to be simple is becoming more complex due to information overload. That's where you step in to guide them. It is best to find a niche you wish to specialize in, be it Weddings, Cruises, Groups, Europe, Ski and Golf or another topic that interests you.

Getting to know your client is key to making a sale. People will not buy from you until you satisfy their want and desire and you will do so by asking the questions who, what, where, when and how much.

Who is traveling? Single, couple, friends, group (find out what type of group, e.g. students vs. church group)

What are they looking for? Just airfare, a package, cruise, coach tour

Where? Where do they want to go and what do they want to see or do?

When? This will help you decide the season as well as the product. If someone wants a cruise in January, for example, you wouldn't offer them an Alaskan cruise.

Seasonality
Typically travel falls into the dates below

Peak Season
Everywhere from 15th of Dec to 15th of Jan – Christmas
From 14th of Mar to 28th of Mar – March Break

High Season
Caribbean - From 15th of Jan- Until the week after Easter
Europe - From 15th of Jun to 15th of Sep

Shoulder Season
From 01st May to 01st of Jun and from 16th Sept to 15th Oct

Low Season
other times

Budget - This is **very** important to find out from the start as you need to find out whether you are looking for a 2 star or 4 star property, combined with the seasonality to see what you can recommend in their price range. Same goes with Motor Coach Tours as to the number of days and inclusions, airfare the class and duration, etc.

Pricing - Something that may surprise you is all wholesalers sell to all agencies at the same cost however not all wholesalers get the same rate from the supplier. For example, to make up a package you need airfare, hotel and transfers. Say ABC has a package from Boston to Las Vegas staying at The Luxor , for 7 nights at $800 USD, based on double occupancy. Agency DEF offers the same product but uses a different airline and their cost is $900USD for all agencies. The difference is that each wholesaler negotiated their contract based on the supplier and how many seats/rooms they could bring to them. All agencies do not receive the same rate of commission, however. The commission is where you make your money.

So why are there so many different prices offered for the same product you ask? The obvious answer is the agency discounted it from their commission however there are other ways to offer a lower price. Some examples would be booking a group departure (10 rooms or more generally), having past passenger rates for cruises if they have sailed with them before, having AARP or CARP (Associations of Retired Persons), regional discounts as well as some hotels offer the 3rd or 4th night free with some suppliers.

It is **very** important to read the small print by any advertised price to see what the price is including. Check how many people are required in a room; check if they are calculating a child rate (ages 2-11 generally, however some are to 17) , what type of room it is and what's included, and finally are there any additional taxes or resort fees included.

You will need to understand some lingo that is used in the industry and what it means.

Wholesaler - a company who buys bulk space and packages to resell to Travel Agents and their clients.

Supplier - the company providing the service

Sked Change - schedule change normally for air travel

UC - not confirmed

KK - confirmed from waitlist

Minimum Connect - the minimum connecting time where they are changing planes

Waitlisted - something you have requested was sold out and waiting for someone to cancel or space to become available

CRS - computer system you are using, Sabre and Apollo are the main two

Queue - send a file to a wholesaler's computer; also where you check for messages from the airline in your computer system

City Codes -   Three letters that correspond to an airport - see separate listing

Consolidator - A company that negotiates special rates with the airlines in exchange for sending them business.

Commission - a percentage of the sale you receive from a travel sale from the wholesaler, or supplier.

IATA - the governing body over airline tickets. Each agency who issues their own tickets require an IATA number

2
City Codes

- USA and Canada
- International and Sun Destinations
- Documentation

.

Every airport in the world has a three letter code to identify it. You can easily consult your **BONUS**, located at www.priortotakeoff.com, however some main ones have been added below that you should be aware of. All Canadian airport codes start with Y.

YYZ, YTZ - Toronto, Canada
YUL, YMX - Montreal, Canada
YOW - Ottawa, Canada
YYC - Calgary, Canada
YVR - Vancouver, Canada

USA
BOS - Boston, USA
DCA, IAD, WAS - Washington DC, USA
SEA - Seattle, USA
LGA, JFK, EWR - all service NYC, NY, USA
LAX - Los Angeles, USA
SFO - San Francisco, USA
SAN - San Diego, USA
PHX - Phoenix, USA
PHL - Philadelphia, USA
PIT - Pittsburgh, USA
MCO - Orlando, USA
TPA -Tampa, USA
RDU - Raleigh, USA

ORD - Chicago, USA
LAS - Las Vegas, USA
JNU - Juneau, Alaska

Europe/Asia
AMS - Amsterdam, Netherlands
MAD - Madrid, Spain
CDG - Paris, France
LHR, LGW - London, UK
VCE - Venice, Italy
FCO - Rome, Italy
BCN - Barcelona, Spain
LIS - Lisbon, Portugal
TLV - Tele Viv, Israel
SIN - Singapore, Singapore
CPH - Copenhagen, Denmark
DUB - Dublin, Ireland
PEK - Beijing, China
TYO - Tokyo, Japan
BKK - Bangkok, Thailand

Sun Destinations
AUA - Aruba
POP - Puerto Plata, DR
PUJ - Punta Cana, DR
VRA - Varadero, Cuba
NAS - Nassau, Bahamas
MBJ - Montego Bay, Jamaica
GCM - Grand Cayman

STT - St Thomas, USVI
SJU - San Juan, Puerto Rico
SJO - San Jose, Costa Rica
BZE - Belize City, Belize
SXM - St Martin
SKB - Saint Kitts
CUN - Cancun, Mexico
PVR - Puerto Vallarta, Mexico

It is necessary to double check where your clients want to go as there can be the same city names in more than one country. For example there is Kingston, Canada and Kingston, Jamaica as well as Sydney Australia and Sidney, Canada. You wouldn't be the first person who has sent their client to the wrong country! That brings me to another point. You need to make sure your client has the right documentation to enter the country they are travelling to. A good rule of thumb is their passport is valid at least 6 months after their return. You can get this by using your **BONUS** located at www.priorto takeoff.com, or you can check in your CRS. You also must check their citizenship status. Are they landed immigrants status; Will they need a re-entry visa?

3
Runway Decode

- Understanding an Airline Ticket
- Understanding Fares
- Schedule Changes

There aren't too many agencies that issue their own airline tickets these days unless you work for a large agency doing great volume. Very few airlines pay commission anymore. Regardless, you will need to know how to deal with airline tickets to ensure the tickets the consolidator sends you are correct and to speak to the airlines, if necessary.

The ticket number always starts with the three numbers assigned to that airline.

Locator - Is usually five letters (may contain numbers too depending on CRS used to book it)

Class - The class of service booked...F-first J, C-business, Y,M,B,Q,V,K, X, S- economy

Take a look at the ticket on the next page. It is an *open jaw* ticket between LAX and SFO as they travelled another way not on this ticket. They flew into one city and left from another.

On the next page is a look at a paper ticket. Although the electronic ticket is more commonly used now, it will familiarize you with all the necessary fields and what they look like.

1. Name of passenger
2. Airline it was ticketed over. Note- The agency issuing the ticket requires a plate from that airline. If it does not have their plate it can be issued over another airline in certain conditions.
3. Exchange rate at time of ticketing
4. Endorsements- tells you if there are restrictions on the fare
5. Date
6. Sold inside, ticketed inside country ticket validated to. Also the airline locator just below that.
7. Validation of ticket
8. City pairs (Moscow to/from Prague)
9. Taxes
10. Total fare in local currency

The fare breakdown is in the center of the ticket just after the USD amount and starts with 16OCT98. By looking at that you can see MOW (Moscow) SU (Aeroflot) to Prague was 1 90.00 and back to MOW was 190.00 making the total NUC 380.00 (NUCS are usually equivalent to the USD) and the ROE (Rate of Exchange was 1.00000) If you look in the fare box you will see the USD amount is indeed 380.00.

Fare Basis

Have you ever noticed people pay different fees to change their tickets? This is because of the fare they originally paid and it's restrictions. The lower they pay, the less flexible the ticket is, generally. People who are travelling for business need the extra flexibility as they are forever changing their tickets, for example; when their meeting is canceled or ends early you wouldn't want to have sold them a non- refundable, non- changeable ticket at the lowest price. By the way, a changeable ticket and transferable ticket are two different things. Seldom can you transfer a ticket to another party, yet usually you can change the ticket to another time or date for a fee. Each case is different as to how sure they are about the times and dates you are booking. It is important to read the rules of the fare you are selling them and communicate them to your client. These are found in your CRS when you ask for all fares available from the two city pairs (the three letter code for the origin to the three letter code for the destination). If they need lots of flexibility you normally would book B, M or Y class to allow for that. You can sometimes book Q, V or K class but you need to tell them what the fee is every time you change it. The rule also tells you valid connecting points, if stopovers are permitted and where, how long the fare is valid for and seasonality. The AEROFLOT ticket on the previous page had a fare basis that read **KRX3M**. What this fare basis tells us even before looking at the rule is it is booked in K class (the first letter as an indicator), it is a return ticket as indicated by the R, X means it is valid for midweek travel (Sun-Thurs, would be a W if was a weekend) and the maximum stay is three months as is indicated by the 3M. Something else to note: if there were more cities on the ticket, you would see an X (connection) or O (stop) in the column to the left of the city indicating whether it is a connection or a stopover. A stopover is more than four hours in a city. A connection is usually less than 4 hours and includes a change of planes.

Schedule Changes

Schedule changes can be your worst enemy or a blessing in disguise.

Depending on how much change there is in the flight time, it can lead to disconnecting flights at connecting points, not enough connecting time due to schedule changes and more. While each airline has their own policy, generally if the change is more than three hours or is operating on a different day, you can use this to your advantage as it will allow you to change dates as well as times at a higher fare level. You must call into the airline to check the policy on this particular schedule change. If the change is under three hours and does not pose a problem on the original itinerary, there is little you can do, unfortunately.

.

4

Popular Places to
Let Your Hair Down

• Introduction to many destinations
• Where to dive
• Where hurricanes don't hit

There are so many destinations to travel to, here is a word or two about each to get you started and you can consult your **BONUS** for more detailed information and suggested chain hotels.

AUA - Aruba – only island outside hurricane belt (June-Oct)

POP - Puerto Plata, Dominican Republic - good value, no or low single supplements; programs for kids

PUJ - Punta Cana, Dominican Republic - good value, nice beaches; kids programs at most

VRA - Varadero, Cuba-many Cuban resorts low or no single supplement; nice beaches; food not the greatest; good value

NAS - Nassau, Bahamas – can be expensive if not all inclusive; nice beaches; duty free shopping

MBJ - Montego Bay, Jamaica – nice beache;, plantations

GCM - Grand Cayman- can be very expensive to eat; good for scuba or snorkeling; quiet island; upscale; shipwrecks

STT - St Thomas, US Virgin Islands – good duty free shopping

SJU - San Juan, Puerto Rico- lots of history; good for surfing

SJO - San Jose, Costa Rica – good for nature enthusiasts; beaches vary; cloud and rain forests

BZE - Belize City, Belize – also good for nature

SXM - St Martin – duty free shopping; half Dutch and French island

SKB - Saint Kitts - laid back; not too common

CUN - Cancun, Mexico – nice beaches, close to Mayan ruins, close to Mayan Riviera; another beautiful resort area

PVR - Puerto Vallarta, Mexico - quaint town; check for travel warnings

UVF - St Lucia- beautiful, great for bird watching; mountainous

PTY - Panama City, Panama- nice beaches; Panama Canal

YYZ, YTZ - Toronto, Canada- close to Niagara Falls; CN Tower

YUL, YMX - Montreal, Canada- French; cafes

YOW - Ottawa, Canada- Capital of Canada, Parliament

YYC - Calgary, Canada- gateway to Rockies

YVR - Vancouver, Canada- many Alaska Cruises leave from here; on Pacific Ocean

BOS - Boston, USA – gateway to Cape Cod; on Atlantic Ocean

DCA, IAD, WAS - Washington DC, USA- Capitol of USA; White House

SEA - Seattle, USA – nice coastal city; some Alaska cruise ships leave from here; on Pacific Ocean

LGA, JFK, EWR - all service NYC, NY, USA – New York City; Statue of Liberty; Ground Zero

LAX - Los Angeles, USA- Beverly Hills; Disneyland; Santa Monica

SFO - San Francisco, USA- close to Napa Valley (wine); Golden Gate Bridge; on Pacific

SAN - San Diego, USA – at border to Mexico; many quaint areas

PHX - Phoenix, USA- golfing; desert

PHL - Philadelphia, USA – history and airline connecting point

MCO - Orlando, USA- Disney World

TPA -Tampa, USA- on Gulf of Mexico; nice area beaches

ORD - Chicago, USA- The Windy City

DEN - Denver, Colorado- skiing; mountains

LAS - Las Vegas, USA – desert; gambling; gateway to Grand Canyon

JNU - Juneau, Alaska – start and end for some Alaskan cruise; wilderness

AKL - Auckland, New Zealand- two islands; sheep; bed and breakfasts

SYD - Sydney, Australia- Opera House; Ayers Rock (Cairns); Gold Coast; Great Barrier Reef

South America - Trekking; Amazon; Galapagos Islands

Europe - History; many different cultures and ways of life.

5
Car Rentals - What to Know

- Tips to get you the best price
- What you cannot do
- What you are covered for

Pickup and drop off at the same location to avoid a drop off fee

Pick the vehicle up and drop off at same time.

To avoid a lot of add on charges check to see what you are covered for by the state automatically

Check with your insurance company to see if you can get a rider to put on your policy to cover rental cars

Check with any credit cards you may have to see if you have coverage with them if you use that card for payment

Make sure they will pay car rental company directly and immediately.

Car companies run out of small cars first. Only book the minimum you would drive as you will likely get a free upgrade anyways.

You cannot drive a car plated in a different country into your own country.

You need to get an International Drivers Permit if you are travelling to a country where there is a language difference. It's best to check the country where you are traveling to.

Look into leases if you need the car long term. These are especially popular in Europe but can also be done in North America.

If you need a car seat you can usually bring one free of charge with the airlines.

If you have a preferred company you deal with, join their Frequent Renter Club to save doing the paperwork each time.

Prepay cars in foreign countries to save money. Check your BONUS for some suggested suppliers.

6
Accommodation

- Room Types
- Meal Pans
- Weddings and Groups

There are all types of classifications when it comes to accommodations, but what do they mean?

If you make a request, the request is never guaranteed as you are not the one providing the services.

Types of Rooms

Run of the House - entry level room
Junior Suite - slightly larger than a regular room
Suite - usually has a separate sitting room

The rooms may still vary based on the location. Rooms that are near stairways or in louder parts of hotel (e.g. near disco) will be less preferred by guests and therefore the will sell it at a lower cost.

The view will also determine the cost. Garden or city view is cheapest, while the oceanfront suite would be the most expensive.

Bedding
Most of the bedding is self-explanatory however, sometimes you will come across descriptions that make no sense. For example, you may ask for a room that will sleep five people however the description will say two twin beds. In that case Google the hotel or call or ask the

wholesaler to verify it for you. It is usually just a difference in language that is causing the issue.

Meal Plans
EP - European Plan, no meals
CP - Continental Breakfast
MAP - Modified American Pan- 2 meals daily
Full Board - Breakfast and lunch and dinner (a term used in Europe)
Almost All Inclusive - as it says but some elements are not unlimited
All Inclusive - all meals and drinks included
Half Board - Breakfast and lunch **or** dinner

All Inclusive Resorts

How is "All Inclusive" rated and why does it vary?

All Inclusive star ratings vary depending on who rated them. For example, you can look online at a hotel that shows being rated as a 4- star yet you see it rated as a 2- star in a brochure or wholesalers website. In the first scenario it was likely rated by the Government of that country and what they expect to see in a 4- star based on their standards.

In the second one, it is being rated as a 2 star because that is the level according to Canadian and US standards. The wholesaler representing that property is looking to rate it lower to avoid complaints and rate it as we see it based on our standard of living. **One thing you must remember, people like to travel but when they get there they want all the conveniences of home and you need to sell it accordingly.** On one of my last trips, I returned to one of my favourite resorts, a 2 ½ star resort, in Cayo Coco, Cuba. I had been going there for about 8 years off and on and when someone there asked me if I would recommend it to a client, my answer was no. There is nothing wrong with the resort but it is widely *rumored* that in Cuba you need to stay at a 4 or 5 star resort because of the food. The food at this resort is fine, you are in Cuba after all, however there are only 2 à la carte restaurants to choose from, the snacks are nothing to write home about, any fancy drink is hard to come by, few water sports, but they have bungalows on the ocean.

How else are All Inclusives and Hotels Rated?
Services Provided
Sports facilities
Number of à la Carte Restaurants
Number of bars
Appeal of Room/ Hotel/Public Areas
Amenities in room
Number of Pools and Hot Tubs
Food taste
Drink appeal and what they offer
Cleanliness

Destination Weddings

Many resorts will offer free weddings with a minimum number of guests/rooms and if you look hard enough there are a few that don't have that requirement. It is necessary to book well in advance by contacting the wedding department of the wholesaler or the hotel directly. You will need to know how many rooms, including guests and the bride and groom, and how many nights as well as if there are any children and their ages. They will want to know if it is a religious or civil wedding. Some other questions they may ask is about flowers, photographer, cake, location (beach vs other hotel location), time, date, when are they arriving in the country (In some places you have to be in the country a certain number of days prior to the marriage), if they will need witnesses, etc.

Groups

Depending on the type of group, you may have special requirements. Will they need meeting rooms and if so, for how many people, Audio/ Visual equipment, seating style, etc. What about catering? How many resort rooms do you need and what area and room type? These are all questions you will need the answer to so your clients will not have an issue on arrival.

7
Cruises

- Cruise Vocabulary
- What's Included
- Itineraries

Here we are, a prime example of when you and your clients can travel for free. Anytime you book and pay for 10 cabins, rooms or seats, you get 1 free. So market to any and all groups you know. The people who are traveling for free still must pay the taxes. You can use this to your advantage because the total for the 40 cabins would typically be $80000 (40x $2000 = $80 000) is now 36x $2000 =$72 000 as four people are now traveling free, bringing the cruise fare to $1800 per cabin… for a savings of 200.00 per cabin. Of course it is not necessary to pass the savings on to the group, you can just go for free or the group leader can go for free, etc.

Words to Know

Port Charges - this is added to the cruise fare to cover the fees the ship pays to stop in at the ports on the itinerary

Ports - Where you stop on the cruise

Day at Sea - No port that day as ship is enroute to next port.

Cabin/Stateroom - where you sleep

Inside Stateroom - no window

Outside Stateroom - has window or porthole (round window)

Eastern Caribbean Itinerary - islands such as St Martin, St Thomas, St Kitts

Western Caribbean Itinerary - Cozumel, Grand Cayman, Jamaica

Southern Caribbean Itinerary - Usually leaves from San Juan and goes to ports such as Aruba, Bonaire etc

Stern - back of ship

Bow - front of ship

Aft - towards back of ship

Starboard - right side of ship when facing forward

Port - left side of ship when facing forward

Past Passenger - traveled with that cruise line before

Cruising is one of the most profitable niches to explore as an agent. Not only do they you receive commission on the cruise but with some cruise lines give commission on shore excursions, drink packages and pre and post hotels as well.

For most people airfare is also required . However, I am not aware of any that offer commission on cruise line airfare, only a net rate (no commission).

Seasickness is a major concern for many potential clients. There have been many improvements to stabilizers on cruise liners so it is no longer a concern for most people. If you still have someone concerned, let them know that they will feel the motion less at sea level. But, don't book them on any Trans Atlantic or major open water cruise at first, including going to Central or South America from the USA. Book an Alaskan, European or Caribbean cruise first. There are also many aids on the market they can buy and take with them just to be sure.

Types

Mega Liners such as Princess, Holland America, Celebrity, Seabourn, Costa, Carnival, etc. These ships are like floating hotels and have pools, spas, wait staff, numerous restaurants, stores, entertainment aboard for the comfort of their guests. They can usually only access larger ports of call due to the size (tonnage) on the ship.

Small Ships - Windstar, Regent, Silverseas, Paul Gauguin, and Yachts of Seabourn are some of the most common ones. These small ships can gain access to almost any port as they are much smaller. However due to their intimate size they may not offer as many amenities. There is a range for small ship cruising starting with the rivers of the USA up to exotic ports so the cost varies greatly.

River Cruising - AMA Waterways, Viking Cruises, American Queen, etc

A part of small ship cruising is that it will get you into small ports along many European rivers instead of having to do a shore excursion to get to the town/city. American Queen is a steamship riverboat that is similar in the USA. **What's included?**

Cruises are such a great value because they include so much! Normally your onboard entertainment, your meals and your accommodations are included. Some cruise lines are now offering drinks included however most have a drink package for purchase

Extra Cost

Some additional costs to be aware of include:

Transfers to/from the Ship from the Airport or Hotel

Gratuities - $1-3 per person for dining, wait and room staff

Drinks - including soft drinks

Shore Excursions - tours at port

Supplements for high-end food at à la carte restaurants on some ships

Anything you purchase onboard or at the Casino, if there is one

8
Rail

- Major Rail Companies
- Rail Passes
- Specialty Trains

Travelling by train is a great way to travel without having to worry about directions, local regulations and hotels enroute. Each country has its own rain system which can be booked point to point or by rail pass. Sleeping accommodations are always additional and range from a berth to a bedroom.

The most common rail companies are the following:

VIA Rail Canada

Amtrak - is the USA rail system

Britrail - Britain's rail system

Eurorail - offer transportation to/from countries in continental Europe

There are also local privately owned tourist trains that operate in certain countries. These include:

The Rocky Mountaineer - does the Rockies area in Canada

The Blue Train - out of South Africa

Palace on Wheels - out of India

Orient Express -Asia

as well as many others

9

Escorted Tours - Motor Coach

- How they are priced
- Pros and Cons
- What's Included

Escorted Tours have many pros and some cons depending on what your client is looking for. They can be the best way to go for some people as they have an escort who is familiar with the area, know where the attractions are, where to stay, where to eat, etc. Some of the cons include a pre planned itinerary which may be too fast/slow paced and you move as a group so you have little independence.

Escorted tours vary in price and depend on what and how much is included. Some things you may want to use as a comparison include:

Number of nights
How many meals are included?
Is air included to and from departure point and also within the tour?
How many and what attractions are included?
Area covered
The star rating of hotels used
Location in hotels ..e.g. city vs airport hotels and places within walking distance
How far to related attractions
Average age of people in group
Are transfers included?
How many nights in each place or hotel?
Is baggage taken care of?

10
Doing the Needful

- What to Include on Invoice
- What to Offer
- What You Need

Some paper work is always involved in all professions, including the travel industry. You need to protect your "ass"ets as they say in this " dog eat dog world". It is best to use this as a checklist for each sale you make to avoid forgetting something.

Always offer insurance. The best one is the all - inclusive with health, cancellation, baggage and air flight accident insurance. If they decline it get them to sign that they have waived it so you have the documentation, if you are challenged.

If your client is booking anything rated under 4 star or with a company that is not preferred, get them to sign a waiver that they are aware of that so they cannot hold you or your company responsible.

Always supply your clients with an invoice within 24 hours and on it state how much they paid, dates of travel, all necessary trip information, anything to be paid locally, and any balance due and the date due.

Give a brochure to your client so they have the wholesaler's terms and conditions at time of booking.

On invoice state what documentation is required for the nationality in your country and state if they have a different nationality that they must get documents needed to travel on their own.

On the invoice, state **"conditions may vary from your home country and you must adjust your expectations as the way of life varies from place to place."**

Any agent selling travel does need **Errors and Omissions insurance** as well as a license to sell insurance from state/province. In some places passing a travel proficiency exam is necessary.

Congratulations you are now well on your way to starting your exciting new career in Travel!

Of course you will need to do your own research as to what area of the world you want to sell and to whom. Familiarize yourself with the destinations, read brochures and jump in. Remember the easiest way to earn a lot of money in this industry is to sell to groups. Cruise, Motor Coach, Wedding Parties, etc. Be sure to check out the bonuses at www.priortotakeoff.com for lots more useful information.

Are you finally ready to earn what you are worth?

About the Author

Although the author is Canadian, Cheryl Cuffe has lived overseas as well as the USA before coming back to Canada to live. Cheryl's career as always been travel related as she got the travel bug early in life.. She also has a touch of humanitarian in her and wanted to help others enjoy the career she has for years without spending thousands going back to school.